Hikikomori

ひきこもり

Hikikomori

poems by
Virginia Aronson

art by
Rose-Ann San Martino

SHANTI ARTS PUBLISHING
BRUNSWICK, MAINE 04011

Hikikomori

Published by Shanti Arts Publishing

Cover and interior design
by Shanti Arts Designs

Shanti Arts LLC
Brunswick, Maine
www.shantiarts.com

Printed in the United States of America

ISBN: 978-1-951651-92-3 (softcover)

Library of Congress Control Number: 2021939685

For all who have spent
too much time alone in their room

"What is the Japanese soul, what is the Japanese heart?"

—Koichi Kato,
Liberal Democratic Party leader

"Why do people have to be this lonely? What's the point of it all? Millions of people in this world, all of them yearning, looking to others to satisfy them, yet isolating themselves. Why? Was the earth put here just to nourish human loneliness?"

—Haruki Murakami,
Sputnik Sweetheart

Contents

Hikikomori

Even before the virus
I pulled inward
as the Japanese say
hikikomori
my choice
my self
a boy inside a man
a girl not a woman
a child not an adult
alone in my small room
bed on the floor
desk on the floor
trash and clothes piles
scattered dust bunnies
as familiar
as friends
no one else sees
or says, teases
encourages, pushes, demands
or judges me, my books
in teetering stacks
alphabetized, arranged
phone, tablet, laptop
Mother's neat trays of food

ignored
in favor of easy-to-eat
single serving bags
chips, noodles, cookies
my teeth unbrushed, hair
long, damp, tangled
no bath for days that blend
into weeks, months, a year

I have been here, self-
imprisoned free
to be
whatever, whoever
I am
in the room
I slept in
as a child with dreams
of love, career, travel
gone now
crushed by the world
mean-eyed, harsh-lipped
cruel and violent
and now the pandemic

showing you too
hikikomori

alone
in your own world
alone
with yourself
your swirling thoughts.

Hikikomori is a Japanese term that translates
to "pulling inward." Literally, to stay in or
withdraw. The noun *hikikomori* is also used
in the verb form *hikikomoru* (ひきこもる). The
root of this verb, which means "to confine
oneself indoors," comes from *hiku* ("to pull
back") and *komuru* ("to seclude oneself").

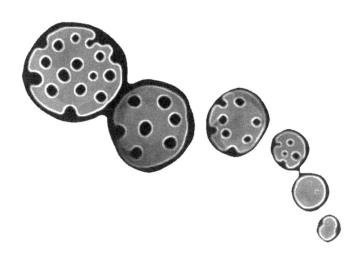

Brave New World

Small as the square blocks
of black and white floor tiles
tight as the smooth plaster
of four whitewashed walls
suffocating as the thick foam
of the single bed mattress
wrinkled white sheets, pillow
warm from a single ray
spring sunshine leaking in
curtained windows to the outside

world where soft pastel light
splashes on rocks, green plants
beach sand, grassy parks
mall shops and sidewalk cafés
the *kombini*, 24-hour store
for bentō boxes
takeout meals

while inside
me
all is silent,
black and white
like in old films, dreams

I sleep through
another day
awaken to darkness
seeping under the door
I refuse to open
my no-takeout box
drab, unchanging
brave as I can be
with no *tatemae*
no public face
only what I allow
to come in

my life.

If someone in Japan becomes a shut-in
and avoids the outside world for more
than six consecutive months, the Japanese
Health, Labor, and Welfare Ministry
labels it a case of *hikikomori*. Japan has
more *hikikomori* syndrome/*hikikomori*
sufferers than anywhere else in the world.
Estimates range from a million to several
million cases. First defined in the late 1990s,
hikikomori is still not well documented.

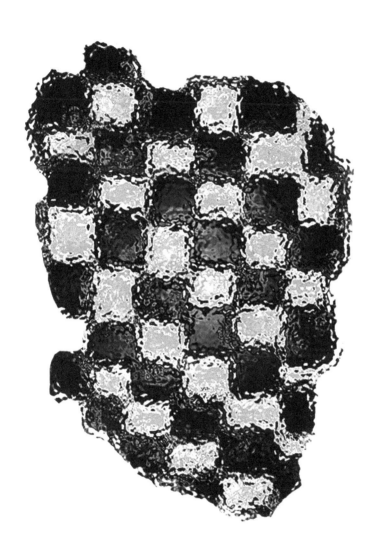

It Can't Be Helped

In a stage play
of meaningless *noh*
I am the only performer
who leaves his mask
hanging off
shikata ga nai.

In rows like army formations
every year, every classroom
students sit, chant
with monotone fervor
me the only soldier
who rolls his eyes, yawns
shikata ga nai.

On crowded commuter trains
the salarymen line up
the women in dark suits
eyes downcast, nails trim
shoes plain, perfectly polished
I am hooded, slouching
shikata ga nai.

Japan is a suicide forest
the people wandering
in the ancient woods
a noose, a knife
to gut the emptiness
spill out on tall grass
under swaying pines, serene
blue skies clouding over
shikata ga nai.

We self-sacrifice daily
bow down to the collective
work, work, work
to please nobody
our lost selves
alone in this gray sea
of turbulent quietude.

A state of being rather than a mental illness, *hikikomori* is linked to the cultural lack of respect for individuality and disregard of those not engaged in education or traditional work. Most *hikikomori* are decent people who happen to find themselves in a difficult situation as Japan confronts serious social and economic problems. These include a lack of jobs for young people, a sharp increase in the average age of the population, and difficulty getting back into the labor force after leaving due to a job change, the need for childcare, or time spent caring for aged parents.

Anime Me

Alone in a room
day after day
all night long
online, offline
I read stories
graphic novels
manga, comic books
one after another
colorful cartoons
Japanese girls, boys
outsmarting and defeating
evil doers, overcoming
obstacles to a good life
winning the war for
personal freedom
beating the odds against
social oppression
that drives us to hide
in our tiny cocoons
alone in a room
day after day
all night long
I create my own action
punch holes in the walls

practice martial arts
draw, write, imagine
heroes in bodysuits
hair flying, capes, expressions
serious, virile, tough
symbols of power fixed
to proud chests, sexy
smiles used to seduce
assimilate, conquer
like Amaterasu, creation myth
sun goddess who took light
into the cave, leaving
the whole world
in darkness.

Japanese young people are vulnerable to the lure of extreme social isolation due to widely accepted and rigid norms, high expectations from parents, and a culture of shame. In the West, young people are living with parents for longer than previous generations due to financial constraints and changing social norms. With the advances in digital technologies that provide alternatives to in-person social interaction as well as the current lockdowns due to the pandemic, *hikikomori* is an increasingly relevant concern worldwide.

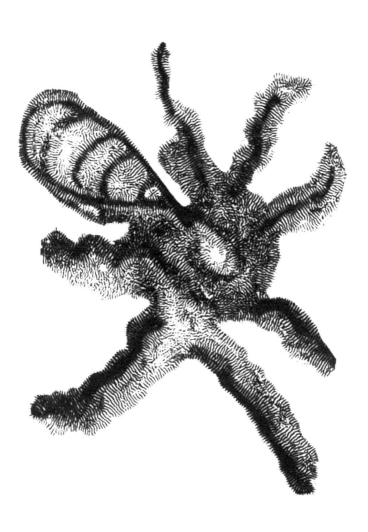

On the Way Out

When my father died
I was still young
in my childhood bedroom
drinking tea, eating snacks
watching TV and reading
all the classics
I wanted
to be a novelist
writing stories
my father mailed
to the literary journals
consumer magazines
big publishing houses.

When my father died
I was still young
naïve and full of myself
big dreams
for a grand future
in which I would star
as the successful son
my parents prayed for
all their lives.

When my father died
I stopped writing
stopped reading
drinking *shōchū*
playing video games
all night long.

When my mother died
I was over forty
lacked self-esteem
locked in my childhood
bedroom
dreamless
alone.

I have forgotten how
to be in the world
scared and scarred
my parents
gone
all their savings
gone
and me
stuck
culture bound.

Hikikomori rely on parents to support them and may have no other close relationships. The typical family is middle or upper income, the *hikikomori* usually their eldest or only son who drops out of school or comes home after experiencing social or job stresses. Instead of seeking therapy, most Japanese parents hide what they see as their own failure to properly parent. Japanese society is worried about "the 80–50 problem," when aged parents begin to die off, leaving behind dependent offspring who have been isolated and financially supported, sometimes for decades.

Homosocial

The mall is packed
with young Japanese
women
women
women
shopping, strolling
Louis Vuitton and Gucci
Louboutin and Lauren
the air redolent
with cherry blossom
perfume
and high-pitched laughter.

The city is busy today
trains and sidewalks
radiant, lively
women
women
women
heading for the office
from their parents' home
from their childhood
bedrooms
simple, elegant

they save on rent
save their wages
for overseas travel
for resort vacations
for designer clothes.

While the Japanese
women, women
are on womb strike
I sit in my dark
womb-like room
thinking of them
living in the present
no future for us

alone.

In previous generations, young single Japanese women were sent to matchmakers for an arranged marriage lest they face a future of isolation, ostracism, and poverty. Today's Japanese women still struggle for gender equality. Career women are responsible for all of the childcare and domestic duties so some are choosing to be "parasite singles" instead, living at home into their 30s and 40s, enjoying a self-focused life without marriage.

My Rental Sister

The letter was kind.
I did not respond.

The letter was funny.
I did not respond.

The email was engaging
personal
revealing.
I emailed her back.

The first visit was brief
we spoke through
my bedroom door
her voice light
as the spring air.

The second visit
the door
remained shut
between us.

Phone calls were rare.
Soon she called me
more often,
then daily.
I missed her
when she didn't
call me back.

One dark winter day
the room cold
my breath gusting
I cracked the door
and we talked
across the threshold.

A few months later
sun warmed us
the door open
all the way
she came inside
all the way
my heart raced
my rental sister

said, "Your life
is exactly

as I pictured,"
and smiled
like that was good.

And me, I asked her
what about me?
My blush hot
on my neck and cheeks.

You too, she said,
her smile more beautiful
than I had imagined.

In Japan, rental sisters and rental brothers
communicate with *hikikomori* clients on
the phone or via letters. With permission,
they will sit outside a closed door while
they try to reassure, befriend, and
eventually coax *hikikomori* out of hiding.
This may take months, even years.

Spirited Away

I would never attack my family
with a crossbow or hunting knife
that I ordered
over the Internet
and hid
in my room
where I am safe
from people who do things
like that.

I would never steal a child
kidnap and keep her
in my room
for company
for it is isolation
from others
in my safe place
that I prefer.

I would never hijack
a bus or a car,
venture out
on the busy streets
to take something

I have no use for
here
in my safe place.

When the therapist asks
if I have violent thoughts
I say no
but
inside I rage
imploding I am
bara-bara
broken apart from others
and captive here
away
from my safe place.

Some desperate Japanese parents employ *hikidashiya*, "those who pull people out." The extraction of the *hikikomori* from the family home can add up to tens of thousands of dollars with repeated attempts and follow-up treatments. For the *hikikomori*, such traumatic events may result in post-traumatic stress syndrome. Parents have been frightened into action, however, after publicized incidences of violence enacted by *hikikomori*, sometimes against their own families.

Invisible

When I walk the gray streets
of the gray city, gray sky
overhead the neon blinkering
like warnings, cheesy memos
flashing in the heavy mist

When I reach for stray thoughts
crowded out
by rote facts
and the paper due
at school tomorrow
the accounts due
at work tomorrow

When I try to analyze
a passage I read
in Kant
I can't
imagine
concepts not given
in classrooms, at home

When I lean in
light rain cool

on my bare neck
my mind afloat
on a haze of *biiru*
I can finally relax
into my real self
honne
compose a song
lyrics, a poem
before old voices
inside me
drown out, drenching me
the sudden downpour
reminding me
I am but one
of the herd, a follower
in a land of followers.

Each time this happens
inside my head
inside my body
kireru, bursts
of boiling hot anger
rising like steam
and what I think then
analyze, compose
is how I might

express my rage
to the expressionless masses
gray faced, in lockstep
accepting of our fate.

In Japan, there is no self separate from
society. School and work are collective
and deny the self rather than enhancing
the ego. Japanese are not taught critical
thinking or encouraged to explore
innermost thoughts and feelings. If you
drop out of school or work, there is no
social context so you are left with no
identity—you are socially invisible. The
suicide rate in Japan is high, as are the
rates of alcoholism, depression, and divorce.
People who are creative and innovative
may leave Japan for an environment
where there is more flexibility and the
opportunity for personal empowerment.

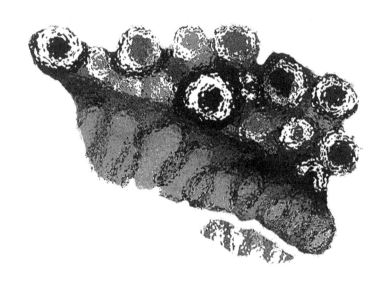

Nomikai

I knew it was not a fit
the job I had worked
my whole life for:
childhood in *juku*
cram school every day
studying, studying
head bent low
under my mother's
angry mouth, father's
disapproving gaze.

College and grad school
grind, grind, stresssssss
and the job market
for dark-suited salarymen
shrinking, shrinking
the pyramid leaving
me: a grain of sand
at the very bottom.

I knew it was not a fit
the long days, evenings
often past midnight
bowing, scraping, rigid

hierarchical culture
low pay and raises
based on seniority.

Also required: *nomikai*
go-drinking meetings
a sleazy bar crawl
women in low-cut dresses
hostesses for hire
overpriced
watered drinks, red-eyed
clients in loose silk ties
ogling, ordering, avoiding
going home

the one place I fit
in with my thoughts
my unique brand
of silent nonconformity.

Hikikomori discover independent thinking and a sense of self the culture does not support. Their isolated lifestyle is a kind of quiet rebellion against conformity, collectivism, and pressures to be successful and perpetuate the status quo. Other rebellious Japanese youth are known as NEET (not engaged in employment, education, or training—estimated to include more than 850,000 young people), *hodo-hodo zoku* or the so-so tribe (younger workers who refuse promotions to minimize stress and maximize free time) and freeters, underemployed by choice and working at low skills jobs in convenience stores, fast food shops, and supermarkets.

Day #3652

Happy anniversary
to me
and me alone
ten years
in my subterranean villa
where day is night
and night is day
my life floating past
on a dark thundercloud.

In other worlds
I am a hero
vanquishing evil
firing endless rounds
protecting lovely maidens.

In other worlds
I am a genius
creating artwork
brilliant commentary
intelligent arguments
problem solving, enlightening
with my visionary concepts.

In other worlds
I am a master
chess
shogi
Sudoku
video games
too many
to name.

In such worlds
I am not
my body
and its needs
its disappointments
I am
only
an all-powerful force.

And if the Earth stops spinning
I'm sure
I won't notice.

An extended period of withdrawal creates a greatly reduced space-time context, so most *hikikomori* reverse the normal day-night routine. With extended isolation, people lose perception of the duration and passage of time. The days go by and are all the same. It's a trap, and it's hard to escape. Changes in lifestyle build slowly and may gradually become virtual; the move to a virtual life might not be fully reversed.

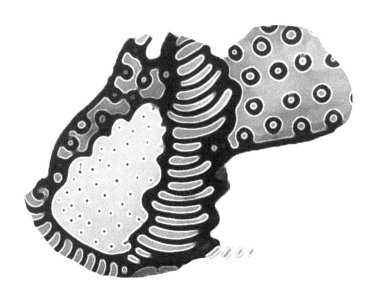

We Are All Hikikomori Now

It starts with the food
delivered to the door
swabbed like ship decks
for germs, threat of death.

It moves on to hibernation
mistings of alcohol
cloth masks, plastic shields
gloves, bleach, and PPEs
to answer the door.

Soon it is hermit style
streaming all night
binge watching
binge eating
binge phoning
contact reduced to pixels
via Zoom, Facetime.

Eventually nobody leaves
commutes
socializes
shops
except online.

Eventually nobody leaves
the walls are built
sakoku, closed country
real life taking place
on the other side.

By then we are alone
shut in, shut down
the *hikikomori* lifestyle
trending, trending.

Virtual reality and live streaming may play an important role in the post-pandemic world as the aversion to close contact will likely linger after the virus is contained. Young people everywhere will be even more vulnerable to impacts arising from precarious employment and economic vulnerability. Serious emotional and financial challenges could result in a dramatic expansion worldwide of the *hikikomori* lifestyle.

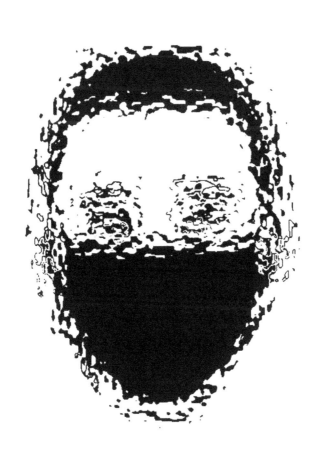

Glossary

bara-bara: broken apart from others; socially separated

biiru: beer

hikidashiya: those who pull people out; those hired to remove *hikikomori* from isolation

hikikomori: a pulling inward; people who isolate themselves to avoid working, schooling, socializing

hodo-hodo zoku: the so-so tribe; made up of younger workers who refuse promotions in order to minimize the stress in their lives and maximize their free time for other activities

honne: one's actual, honest feelings and thoughts; the private self

juku: cram school; supplementary schooling to give students an edge in the fierce competition for placement in schools for lower and high education

kombini: convenience stores

kireru: angry outbursts; sudden explosions of violent behavior

noh: traditional Japanese theater with dance, song, and acting to retell old stories

nomikai: go drinking meetings; after-work time spent with coworkers, bosses, clients, during which alcohol must be imbibed

sakoku: closed off country; former isolationist policy of Japan

shikata ga nai: it can't be helped

shōchū: an ancient Japanese distilled liquor currently trendy with young people

shogi: Japanese chess

tatemae: public face; the self you show to the world

References

Blair, Gavin. "In Japan, extreme bids to help *hikikomori* are causing them further distress." *This Week in Asia* (June 27, 2020).

Butet-Roch, Laurence. Photography by Maika Elan. "Pictures reveal the isolated lives of Japanese social recluses." *National Geographic* (February 16, 2018).

Goodyear, Jason. "*Hikikomori*: identifying extreme social isolation around the globe." *BBC Science Focus* (February 12, 2020).

Lam, Donican. "What Japan's *hikikomori* can teach us about self-isolation." *Kyodo News* (April 25, 2020).

Loesch, Cailin. "They have mastered the space and their emotion: Maika Elan on photographing reclusive Japanese *hikikomori*." *Musée* (March 12, 2018).

McKirdy, Andrew. "The prison inside: Japan's *hikikomori* lack relationships, not physical spaces." *Japan Times* (June 1, 2019).

Zielenziger, Michael. *Shutting Out the Sun: How Japan Created its own Lost Generation.* Vintage, 2006.

About the Author

Virginia Aronson is the author of the chapbooks *Itako* (Clare Songbirds Publishing, 2020) and *Tropical Diagnoses* (Finishing Line Press, 2011). She is the director of FNR Foundation, which published *Mottainai: A Journey in Search of the Zero Waste Life* (Dixi Books, 2019). FNR supports nonprofit organizations that work to improve the broken food system and make healthy food available to all or teach ways of feeding and eating that are good for the earth.

About the Artist

Rose-Ann San Martino studied drawing and painting at the Corcoran School of Art. Her work has been shown in group and solo exhibitions and is held in private collections. She provided illustrations for *The Journey from Oz*, a self-help book on depression, and has taught art classes in North Carolina, where she lives with her artist husband, several chickens, and some rambunctious cats. www.roosterpix.com

Shanti Arts

Nature · Art · Spirit

Please visit us online
to browse our entire book catalog,
including poetry collections and fiction,
books on travel, nature, healing, art,
photography, and more.

Also take a look at our highly
regarded art and literary journal,
Still Point Arts Quarterly, which
may be downloaded for free.

www.shantiarts.com

CPSIA information can be obtained
at www.ICGtesting.com
Printed in the USA
BVHW091713250621
610384BV00017B/1412

9 781951 651923